Carving Horses in Wood

Eric Zimmerman

**Home
Craftsman
Series**

 Sterling Publishing Co., Inc. New York
Distributed in the U.K. by Blandford Press

This work is dedicated to my good friend,
E. J. Tangerman, who inspired the whole thing.

He who works with his hands is a laborer,
He who works with his hands and head is
an artisan,
He who works with his hands, his head and
his heart is an artist.
———Author unknown

There is something about
the outside of a horse
That is good for the inside
of a man.
———Liam O'Flaherty

Edited and designed by Barbara Busch

Library of Congress Cataloging in Publication Data
Zimmerman, Eric.
    Carving horses in wood.

    (Home craftsman series)
    Includes index.
    1. Wood carving—Technique.   2. Horses in art.
I. Title.   II. Series.
TT199.7.Z55   1983   731.4'62   83-414
ISBN 0-8069-7706-X (pbk.)

Copyright © 1983 by Sterling Publishing Co., Inc.
Two Park Avenue, New York, N.Y. 10016
Distributed in Australia by Oak Tree Press Co., Ltd.
P.O. Box K514 Haymarket, Sydney 2000, N.S.W.
Distributed in the United Kingdom by Blandford Press
Link House, West Street, Poole, Dorset BH15 1LL, England
Distributed in Canada by Oak Tree Press Ltd.
℅ Canadian Manda Group, P.O. Box 920, Station U
Toronto, Ontario, Canada M8Z 5P9
Manufactured in the United States of America

CONTENTS

INTRODUCTION

Good Medicine

Men have whittled for decades. Some work on the bench at the country store, some while standing around waiting for the evening local to arrive with visitors and salesmen, and still others at a table, executing their prepared plans in detail. All are experiencing a great form of therapy by exerting varying degrees of mental effort.

These pages indicate the therapeutic value derived from the mental discipline required for whittling or carving a planned project.

As the work develops, more and more concentration is demanded, and a higher degree of communication between mind and hands instinctively takes place. The quality of workmanship found in the finished article is directly related to the degree of creativity in the whittler or carver. Later we will discuss the more creative forms of carving.

Fig. 1. (opposite page). An early collection of horses, made from about 1949 until 1955. Many lack the detailed refinement of more recent models.

HOW IT BEGAN

In 1949, our community held a sesquicentennial celebration, and my company talked me into entering a Conestoga wagon and team of horses in a parade. During the restoration of the wagon, my interest increased to the extent that I made a scale model in full detail. When asked where the horses were, I set out to make a series of tracings for the individual units of the team and, after sawing out a profile of each, soon carved them into shapes to complete the set. Thus, a long series of carved horses was started, which covered a period of more than twenty years.

These first horses were in a quiet standing position, and the urge naturally arose to carve more active beasts. Having had a continual interest in horse motion, rhythm, conformation and general contour through studies involving both still and motion pictures, it naturally followed that some of this latent knowledge would serve as a basis for an unlimited series of designs. Over eighty-five models have been produced since.

The four horses were made of white pine, easy to cut. They were the first of many horses to be eventually cut. Note that each is slightly different, as to a leg or head position. The body shape is generally the same on each, but by tracing each one, I could alter the leg and head position to add interest. In several cases, wood was left between the feet.

The Conestoga wagon model is complete in every detail (Figs. 2 and 3), with small pinheads used as bolts; hinged wagon ends and toolboxes; built-up wheels with hub, spokes and rims; removable tongue

Fig. 2. Conestoga
Wagon.

and double-tree and authentic top cover. The wagon bed is about 6½ inches long.

The axles were made from bicycle spokes, and the wheel nuts were made from the threaded insets which hold the spokes in the bicycle wheel rim. The prevailing motion of the wagon is forward, so the threading of the axles must be cut to turn the nut in a forward direction, and the wheel turning forward keeps the nut tightened. The metal hardware was made of ⅜-by-⅛-inch thin copper, drilled with a No. 64 bit. These were angles, brackets, and cleats. The top hoops were made from ⅛-inch-wide strips cut from a tongue depressor, which had been steamed for hours and bent to shape.

Fig. 3. The wagon chassis is complete and workable to scale. The brake assembly is fixed, but the front-wheel assembly can be disassembled; the tongue, double-tree and wagon-bed cradle can come apart.

7

The best way to build the wheels, I found, is to start with a good straight-grain hardwood (tongue depressors are perfect), then determine the diameter and multiply by pi (3.1416) to get the circumference. Then select a wheel to be copied, count the spokes and divide the linear measurement into equal spaces to accommodate the number of spokes. Plot the detail parts on paper. Make a hub with a hole for the axle rod and cut a groove around the center line of the hub. This is for the spokes which will be slightly tapered and fit tightly when assembled. Boiling the wagon rim strips, or giving them an alcohol treatment will make the wood pliable and able to bend into a complete circle for the tire. Taper each end to fit and glue in a slight overlap. You will learn from trial and error how to finally get a wheel made.

Fig. 4. Wagon with horses, shown as it might appear at a rest stop.

Figs. 5. & 6. Here are the original sketches from which the horses in Fig. 4 were carved. There were no difficulties with anatomy except for the one with its head turned.

Preliminary Studies

In my experience with horse carving, I learned early that some general and comparative knowledge was essential. Therefore, I took my cameras and notebook to the steeplechases and other horse shows and made stills and motion pictures (including slow-motion). I also acquired a few books on horses, from Frederic Remington to An'n Alcock. From the pictures I soon learned about breeds, characteristics, relative sizes and shapes, and background history.

The preliminary material shown here is not the complete story of the world of horses, but represents most of the basic elements of the family of horses that I have found useful in the work that I have done. A bibliography is also included to acknowledge the source of part of the

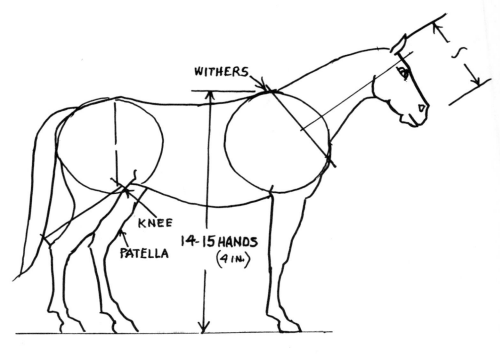

WITHERS

KNEE

PATELLA

14-15 HANDS
(4 IN.)

Fig. 7.

information I have accumulated. This material is intended for the carver who has some basic experience in cutting wood. There are many books written for the beginner.

General blocking-out and setting proportions are indicated in Figs. 7–10. Fig. 7 shows what is done over and over to begin some kind of silhouette for a standing horse, this horse is a thoroughbred. Note that most of the measurements of the horse's framework are based on the length of the head.

To measure the height of the horse, a reference is made to a number of hands. The average man's hand is four inches wide and this is the unit of measure for height. Example: 14 hands is 56 inches (measure to the top of his shoulder).

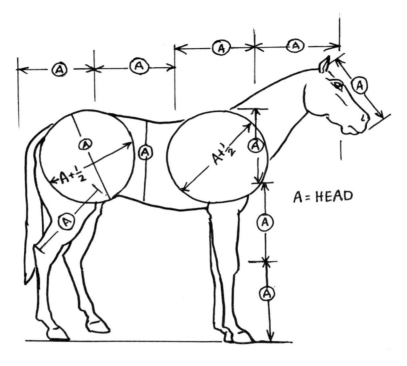

Fig. 8.

Proportions

Every breed of horse has some variations in proportions and dimensions. Fig. 9 provides some guidance, especially in classes such as hunters and saddle horses. There is a great difference between sizes of horses, the tallest and largest being the Shire, and the smallest, outside of special breeding, is the Shetland. The Shire averages about 17 hands high and the Shetland averages about 30 inches or 7 hands + 2 inches.

Other general notes on proportions and characteristics are shown in Figs. 10–16. Here again Figs. 8 and 14 suggest a few practice exercises. Too many of these cannot be made to get the basic shape started.

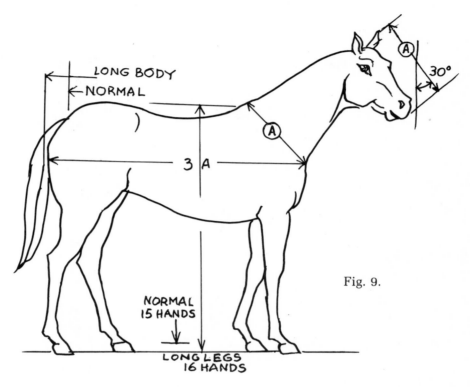

LONG BODY

NORMAL

3 A

NORMAL
15 HANDS

LONG LEGS
16 HANDS

30°

Fig. 9.

To the uninformed, all horses may look alike, but a little reading and a little study will soon reveal the distinct characteristics and relative shapes of various breeds and classes.

To someone who has looked through the various horsemen's magazines, it will be noted that most photographs of Quarter Horses are taken from behind at an angle. This is purposely done to show the muscular rear quarters. Most Thoroughbreds, Tennessee Walkers, and saddle horses have very trim rear quarters. The muscular rear quarters are the notable characteristic of the Quarter Horse, which enable it to make quick powerful starts. This is why they make great cutting horses on a ranch.

Another interesting point that is illustrated from these notes is the difference between the shape of the body at the chest and at the loin. The front of the chest carries the deepest portion of the rib cage and is

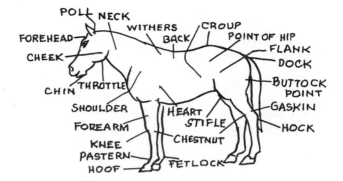

Fig. 10. Parts of the horse.

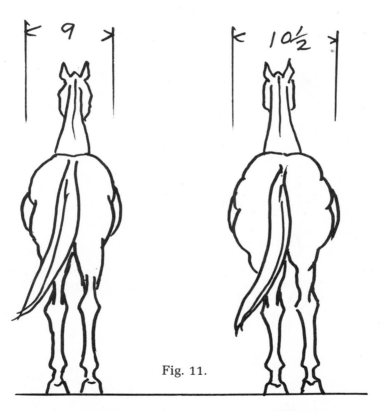

Fig. 11.

THOROUGHBRED   QUARTER

SADDLE
THOROUGHBRED
STANDARDBRED

ARAB
AKHAL TEKE

MORGAN
TENNESSEE

Fig. 12.

oval, or egg-shaped, and at the back of the rib cage, or the loin, it is more nearly round. It can be repeated again that these notes are merely guidelines. As one gets more familiar with the shape of horses, one learns that no two horses are exactly alike, and there is some variation of shape within the breed itself.

Fig. 13. Yearling.

Fig. 14.

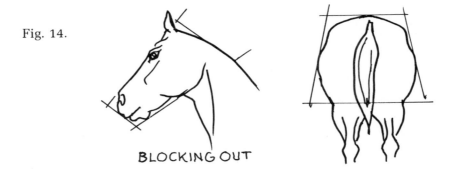

BLOCKING OUT

General proportions for the larger breeds are shown in Figs. 15, 16, and 17; the smaller breeds are shown in Figs. 18 and 19. More extensive descriptions of these will be found later in the section devoted to the various breeds.

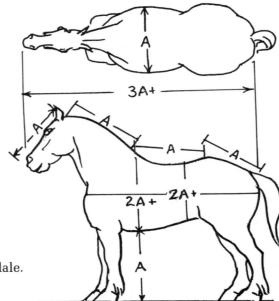

Fig. 15. Clydesdale.

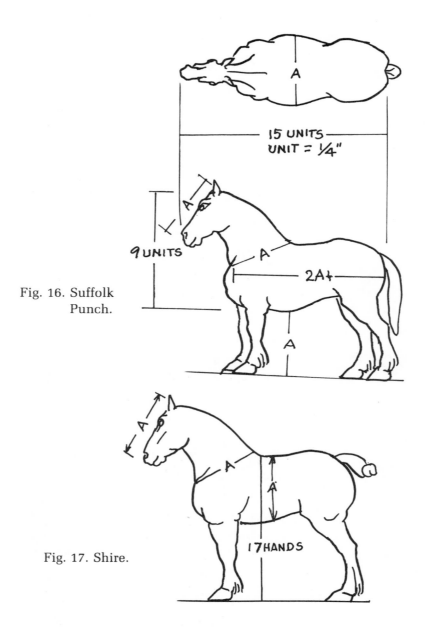

15 UNITS
UNIT = 1/4"

A

9 UNITS

A

2A+

A

Fig. 16. Suffolk
Punch.

A

A

A

17 HANDS

Fig. 17. Shire.

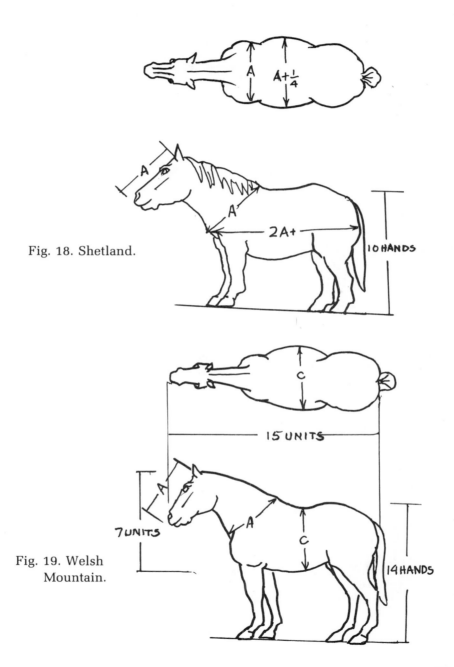

Fig. 18. Shetland.

Fig. 19. Welsh
    Mountain.

17

HOW DO YOU START?

You start at the beginning—with sketches and drawings. Not everybody is equipped with ability to draw and outline freehand. When this ability is lacking, try to trace something you like, and if it's too small or too large, get a photostatic copy which may be an enlargement or a reduction. At least, provide yourself with some kind of a profile drawing as Figs. 20 and 21. These are all preliminary to the model shown in Fig. 22. If it is not quite what you want, trace it and make some modifications which are closer to your requirements.

The next step is to trace or transfer this outline to the block of wood

Fig. 20.

Fig. 21.

and it is ready for the band saw or hacksaw to cut a wood profile of your model. Now you cut away all the material you don't need and you have a finished model. All the finished work in this book shows that I did just that.

The Completed Model

This very fine model (Fig. 22), a thoroughbred mare and foal, illustrates the quality of carving and finishing that is possible after considerable experience. The wood is cherry, and it was a joy to carve because of the

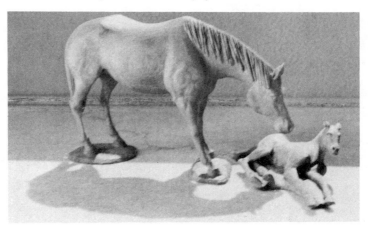

Fig. 22.

firmness of the close grain. Like most hardwoods, this one retained the sharp edges of hair, ears, feet and tail detail. The set required about 70 hours of almost symmetrical modelling. Most of the concentration was spent on producing good proportion and dignity of stance.

Copies and Tracings

When a print or photograph is to be copied for a full-round or bas-relief carving, it should be traced and transferred to the wood. Should enlargement or reduction be desired, the profile sketch should be blocked off in ¼-, ½-, or 1-inch squares and the corresponding enlarged or reduced squares should be prepared. Each section can then be pencilled in, reproducing the proportionate shape in each square. The finished job will be an enlargement of the original (Fig. 23). An easier way is to have a photostatic enlargement or reduction made and prepared for transfer to the wood.

I have made many by each method, but most of mine are development sketches, which started with some original idea, and were followed up with variations until the desired profile was produced.

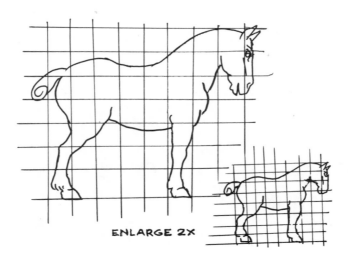

ENLARGE 2X

Fig. 23.

Typical of one of the methods of enlargement is the exercise shown in Fig. 23. This should be practiced on any number of outlines, and it can be enlarged three or four times, as desired. By doing it in reverse, a large image can be reduced.

Fig. 24 is an exact portrait. No originality was required, so it was traced from a photograph of a saddle horse, Capers. A good likeness was made from light mahogany in bas-relief. The carved model was mounted on plywood panelling wood and made up into a fine portrait. The composition of the ears and the vertical neck posture indicate that Capers was "acting up" and standing on his hind legs.

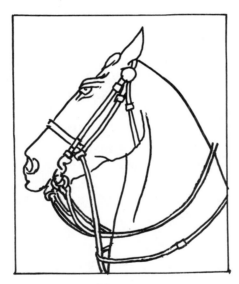

Fig. 24.

WOODS

Wood Has Character

One of the first things that should be understood in carving wood is the character of the various kinds. In the process of sharpening up on some knowledge of woods, I worked on most of them, from soft balsa to maple and walnut burl.

In working with balsa, one is reminded of the mushy, infirm and undecided nature of some people you deal with. Likewise, hard walnut or maple reminds one of the firm, straightforward and positive nature of some other people. Also, the cantankerous, unpredictable nature of marcel-waved buckeye reminds one of similar characteristics in still other people. Yes, woods, like people, have distinctive character, and you must deal with each according to its nature.

Fig. 25. Here are some faces I feel match the various types of wood.

White pine, balsa and soft mahogany are easy to cut, with no great resistance to the hand pressure. Some walnut, manzanita and maple are very hard and laborious during the rough cutting, but they are a real pleasure in the finishing stages. The firmness and smoothness of the grain and the even cellular structure graciously accept the sharp edge of the knife, giving up the small finishing chips with smooth integrity.

Preservations, or coatings, are limited to liquid wax for filling the pores and maintaining the original color, and oil, if a deeper richness is desired, as on Honduras mahogany, manzanita or teak. I like the wood itself and want no finish to come between the material and the observer.

Unusual Woods

An unusual piece of wood came from the butt end of a walnut tree that was quarter-sawn at the root structure. Some of my models were cut from this piece and had extreme contrasts of grain pattern and hardness. This provided some very intriguing cutting challenges and added interest to the finished appearance, Fig. 26.

Fig. 26.

Here is a good example of an Arabian horse (Figs. 26, 27, and 28), with arched neck, sensitive features and prancing feet. Fig. 27 is one of the profile drawings selected to transfer to wood for cutting. Note the selected angle of grain direction. The two free legs need all the strength available, of course, causing mostly cross-grain cutting of the main body contour. Most of the body and legs are completed before separating the free legs from the base. In finishing them, use the fingers gently to back up the ankle and hoof parts as well as for detailing fetlocks and shoes.

The slight forward motion causes the figure to take on the general shape of a parallelogram with unequal angles—a proportion of about 3.3:2.0.

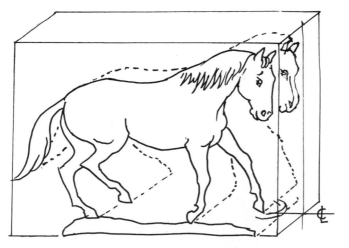

Fig. 27. After the outline of the desired shape is transferred to the block of wood the outline is sawed out with a band saw. The dotted lines indicate the resulting cut-out portion of wood to be carved, beginning with the shaping of the base on the center line.
The thickness of the wood should equal the widest part—the belly.

Fig. 28. Front.

Still another unusual piece of manzanita came from California. It isn't too different except for a deep red color when oiled. My big trouble came when a hind leg of a horse, which was in a cantering

Fig. 29.

motion, separated in three parts through the hoof and partway into the leg. Some internal disintegration, not noticed earlier, had caused the extraordinary situation. I wired the parts together, cut for a while, changed the position of the wrapped wire, and cut some more. When the three parts were glued together, all the long hours of work up to this point were salvaged. (See Figs. 29 and 30.)

Fig. 30.

On many models, a mistake often requires a slight change of contour or proportion to save the work.

The loping gait of the figure is typical of a Clydesdale whose weight prevents him from being too agile. He is an excellent workhorse and can be trained to clomp-clomp in a trot, drawing a brewery or dairy wagon, and seems to enjoy showing off to a crowd.

The Belgian farm horse, shown in Figs. 31, 32 and 33, was cut from an unusually curly buckeye, which was selected in an effort to produce

Fig. 31.

Fig. 32. Similar to Fig. 27. The desired outline is transferred to the block, the thickness should be about the same as the thickness of the horse's belly, and the shaping starts with the center line of the block.

Fig. 33. Front and rear views.

a model showing great strength and stamina. Powerful muscular contours give the effect of ability to move great loads. I had seen a picture of a similar workhorse with its head turned and decided that it would make an unusual model and would introduce some difficult cutting problems. Much of the cutting was across the grain because of the ornery habit of the curly, marcel-type grain to dip and skip, leaving pockmarks after each knife cut. It required great care and extra time. There is a risk of losing line edges when cutting tail and features.

Cutting between the turned head and body was tedious, difficult enough with normal grain. Several cuts to my left hand delayed this work, but this does happen. Turning the head reduces the proportion to an uninteresting, almost square shape, compensated for by an unusual position.

The curly, amber buckeye wood described was a gift from Ray Cottrell, a one time officer in the Wood Collectors' Society, which is international in its collecting activity. I'm sure Mr. Cottrell did not expect too much from this difficult wood. (What he does not know about wood is of no value at all; his lectures are extremely fascinating.)

A TEAM OF HORSES

I wanted to cut a team of four, matched, but with different leg positions, all running (Fig. 34). I had them hitched to a chariot, which places them as a team, four abreast. They are Arabians with the inherent desire of this breed to move fast with great agility when difficulty arises. The Arabian is very stylish with its fine facial features, its arched neck and its dainty pickup of feet when moving. To produce

Fig. 34. Chariot and horses.

variety in the team, I selected four different woods for color contrast—walnut, white pine, Philippine mahogany, and Honduras mahogany. Now, let us look at the problem of making four matched drawings.

This drawing had been made for another model with the rhythm of motion desired. I reduced it in size and used it for a starter.

Note that the main body line (heavy line) is about the same in all figures. Start moving the head position, change the leg position and swing the tail in a different line and you have it.

Again, tracing the body section, I find yet a different arrangement of the legs and a slightly different angle for the head.

This last one has the neck more extended, the front legs a variation of the top position, and hind legs similar to the top position. I kept tracing and changing slightly until I got what I wanted.

Figs. 35—38.

The extended legs, and the forward motion take on the shape of a parallelogram with unequal angles, with the proportion of 3.5:2.0. I gave myself some basic knowledge of horses in motion through many years of photographing races, steeplechases and hunter trials, normal and slow-motion. The advantage of this study is that many changes in the muscular contour are understood, when legs are extended and contracted. Another helpful thing was a study of the horse skeleton, noting the arrangement of various bones during the horse motion. These mini-models have good detail in the face, feet, hair and tail. They were fun to make, requiring about 100 hours.

TOOLS

Carving itself requires only a few square feet of space, and my toolbox can be carried in my hip pocket. Outside of the band saw for cutting the original profile, the only tools I use are shown here in Figs. 39 and 40.

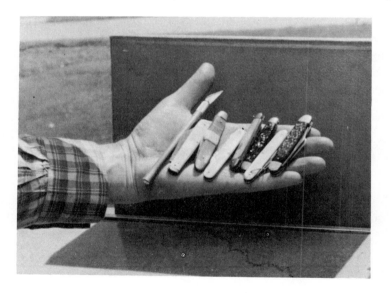

Fig. 39.

All the cutting, except for the fine grooving and details of facial features and hoofs, is outside contour shaping, and the hand knives are the only tools required. In feathering and detailing hair or tail

31

Fig. 40.

strands, I use a sharp point, and draw it along, taking a fine sliver at a time (Fig. 41). With care, some cutting can be done slightly against the grain, especially when forming a curved line.

With proper handling, knives can be directed by the fingers to cut some very fine things. It is the careless and overanxious moment in carving that opens the way for accidental cuts of the hand. One resolves to prevent a recurrence of these things but the drive to make progress overcomes these good intentions and you cut yourself *again*.

Fig. 41.

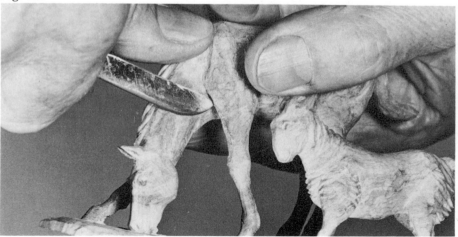

A heavy blade, several small pointed blades, and several large stub-end point blades are all that I need. The secret is keeping a sharp edge. Most of us are guilty of pushing a blade beyond its best cutting edge. As my horses are small, I use no other tools. My hand and fingers provide all the vise, clamps, and stops that I need. More detail on carving tools, types of auxiliary devices, and how to cut wood can be found in E. J. Tangerman's book, *Whittling and Woodcarving*.

Hazards of Whittling

I've often wondered how much the average carver butchers his fingers. It would seem that the person who does most of his work with a pen-knife will frequently put a pretty good nick in his hands, especially the thumb or a finger tip (Fig. 41). When working steadily, I have had my right thumb slit in many places. I've had some serious cuts, several that required dressing and stitching. This can be frustrating, especially if the blood stains a piece of blond wood with some little penetration. Then too, a bandage can create an awkward handling problem when the model is gripped with the left hand. Fig. 41 shows one of the cutting operations that, too frequently, produces cuts.

Fig. 42.

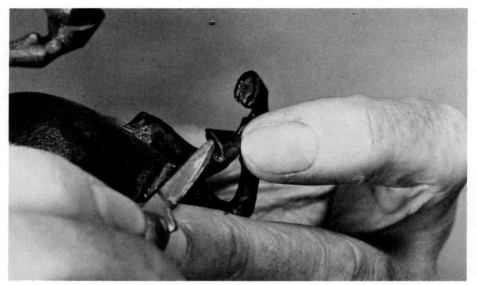

Fig. 43.

In some intricate models, the fingers can be trained to back up such delicate extended unsupported members, as a leg in motion or a flying tail, when the model is a horse. The body is held with the palm and a little finger or thumb, and the other fingers back up a protruding part for careful finishing and detailing (Fig. 42).

For many years, I was frequently in contact with an executive engineer who always inspected my right thumb and several other fingers for slits or scars, and if they were few or almost healed he complained about the inactivity. Once when I ran a large blade into my left hand, he observed the bandaged hand and was pleased, just like the students at Heidelberg University who recognized a scar on the cheek as a mark of honor.

These accidental cuts on the hands are more frequent in carving three-dimensional models. Rarely did I meet with an accident when cutting bas-relief. I have always felt that a cut on the finger or hand soon heals, but a wrong cut in the wood is permanent damage. That is why a dedicated carver takes an accidental cut in stride, especially if blessed with rapid coagulation.

THE HORSE
IN MOTION

This model (Figs. 44, 45, and 46) shows a landing position which causes the rider to leave the saddle and fight for correct balance. It was an interesting model to shape because both rider and horse are in a slightly twisted position; the rider is connected at the boot contact with

Fig. 44.

Fig. 45.

one hand on the neck. The horse is actually on only one foot; the other is connected to wood for support. The wood is Philippine mahogany with a vertical grain which gives strength to the forelegs. The body and neck require cross-grain cutting, but mahogany is not difficult to cut.

Here is a good example of how to keep the forelegs in mind when cutting the hind legs. There is little symmetry in either horse or rider; the axes of shoulders and hips are not parallel. This horse is leading with the left foot. This is important. One must know just where the hind legs are when positioning the front legs. They seldom ever land in pairs.

The horse, in running or jumping, leads with either foot, in a trotting rhythm. The old Currier and Ives prints often show horses with both front and rear legs extended together. This is not accurate. It may seem to be this way when watching a horse race, but in actuality each hoof lands in a 1, 2, 3, 4 succession, usually front left, rear right, front right and rear left, in that order.

Fig. 46. Top and front views.

In planning a horse in motion, the first thing I study is the proper positioning of the feet. Once I have a general design in mind, I study photos and films that I have in order to have each hoof down or up the way they actually are.

After the profile of an animal is sawn out, you must visualize the widest points, such as the hips and belly, and if there is a rider, his or her shoulders and knees. Keeping the wood grain always in mind, start cutting away all the wood that is not needed. Begin with the legs, then thin down the neck and start rounding out the body.

Try to get some expression in the face. Cut in the eyelids and shape the nostrils. With a little experience you will get more than just a slit for eyes and a mere gouge for the nostril. Try to get some detail in the hair and tail. After a little experience, you will begin to cut some hair strands. To do this, take a small, sharp-pointed blade and draw it down time after time until you have a groove that is satisfactory.

Also pay attention to the detail of the hoofs and the fetlocks. These little details are the difference between an ordinary and a quality carving. Observe them in pictures you collect, and you will soon get the feeling of the movement and action of various parts when the horse is in motion.

Fig. 47.

Note that the arrangement takes the general shape of a diamond standing on a point, and must rock either way, in this case forward.

Figs. 47 and 48 show one of the first action models made of light mahogany. In this position the horse has jumped the timber, his fore-legs are preparing to land and his hind legs are neatly picked up to clear the bar. He is supported by a pin through the bar.

The general shaping and detailing is not of the quality of later models. Eyes, nose and ears are rather crudely cut despite the graceful lines of body and legs.

Fig. 48.

Although the profile is all-important in producing a good flow of motion, these action poses demand careful attention to anatomic structure. I am my own severest critic. I have never completed a model that entirely satisfied me. In this case I soon discovered that muscular detail, facial expression and hair and tail lines could be improved. This is why I could not wait until the next one.

One of the most unusual grain patterns was found in this very stylish model made of walnut burl (Figs. 49 and 50). Generally the

Fig. 49.

Fig. 50.

grain runs horizontally to give strength to the extended legs; which were nearly as thin as matchsticks. Several degrees of hardness were found—from soft and even at the top of the head to hard and burly at the belly and legs. This model is well detailed, has good facial expression and is well muscled. Total time required was about 75 hours.

One of the most frequent questions asked by admirers of different models concerns the length of time required for the complete job. Unless one measures the time of each carving session, intense concentration, especially during the finishing stages, causes time to go by unnoticed until several hours have passed. Then a pause for re-evaluation or relaxation may become necessary. I have found that when carving the hind legs of horses in motion I must keep an awareness of what the forelegs are doing, or are about to do. This is where some knowledge of body rhythm, conformation and coordination is essential. One part must always be kept in proportion to every other part.

Discounting the time required, the worth of a carved model can be judged by the kind of communication it makes with the eye of the beholder. All .the fine detail, the well-executed knife-cutting and the elegant proportion of parts mean little to the person with a lack of sensitive judgment. I have seen people select models of lesser carving quality because something in the general appearance appealed to them.

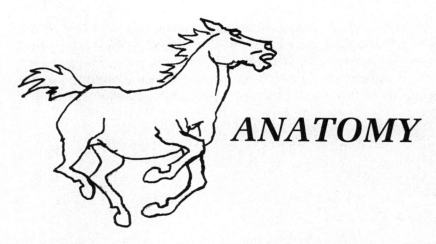

ANATOMY

When seriously carving horses as a specialty, it is impossible to spend too much time reviewing the basic frame structure. Among the devices I have used is a transparent do-it-yourself assembly that I put together some time ago (Fig. 51). It is a good scale model of bone and internal organ arrangement and serves as an excellent reference.

For centuries the horse has been the animal most admired by men. Thus it follows that the graceful motions of a horse in action ought to be

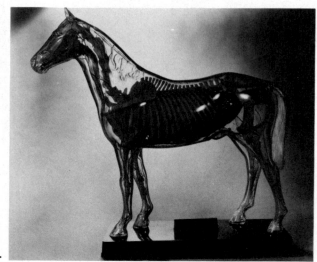

Fig. 51. This assembly kit, The Visible Horse by Revell provides an excellent means for learning horse anatomy.

understood. That is why anyone who takes a special fancy to horses should take some time and learn what happens to his framework when the horse is doing various things.

As stated earlier, many of the older lithographs and prints showing horses racing are not accurate. This was because of lack of observation and study of horse anatomy. In the horse book, *The Golden Book of Horses* by George McMillan, an account is given of the discovery of horse motion through a series of synchronized exposures from several cameras so that actual leg motions can be seen. Because no motion-picture equipment was in existence in 1872, this was the first and only set of pictures taken in series.

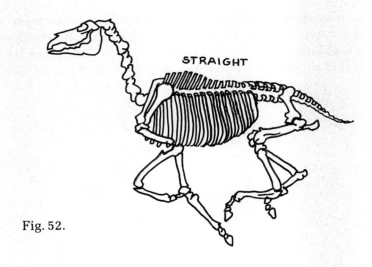

STRAIGHT

Fig. 52.

This exhibit of anatomy shows clearly how a horse's spine remains somewhat rigid and straight (Fig. 52) while he is running. The cat and dog families have spines that will curve, as in Fig. 53, and permit the rear legs to swing forward further, giving them a longer stride. The horse has more powerful rear legs which give him a greater thrust and still provide greater speed.

43

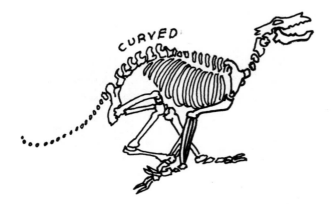

CURVED

Fig. 53.

The thoroughbred, Coaltown, could run at least a quarter of a mile at 49 miles per hour. Man o' War, a powerful winner, had tremendous stride, about 28 feet at top speed. The stride of a walking horse is about 7 feet, which is about the same or slightly more than the length of the body.

BREEDS

Hunter and Steeplechaser

Hunters and steeplechasers are said to be the result of a cross between a thoroughbred and a Percheron that took place long ago. They must be agile, obedient and strong enough to carry weight often for long distances, while clearing fences and obstacles.

    This model (Fig. 54) required the most advanced planning and

Fig. 54.

sketching of any. The red mahogany block, 4 inches thick, was 75 percent wasted in the cutting. To show speed in the jumping horse, and a sudden jolting stop in the fallen one, I felt that one should be nearly symmetrical and the other very asymmetrical. Thus, the fallen horse was not at all in a formal posture. What do the hindquarters do when the body twists and lands on the left shoulder? The horse must be designed with many opposing lines, off parallel, to show violent action. The wood was even-grained and one has a desire to whack at it to get a chiselled look. This one, a real skull session, used up well over 100 hours.

Fig. 55.

Usually a pyramid design is static and quiet, yet this one shows how the action line of the jumping horse is suddenly stopped by the curved neck of the fallen horse. It is not recommended that the beginner try to do this model. There are far too many problems for the novice.

Fig. 56.

Mustang

The world of the mustang was always the open plains. The name is Spanish for "running wild." They were first tamed by the Spanish Moors and brought to Mexico by Captain Cortez in 1519, the first horses to land on the American continent. The Indians made use of them for working and fighting. Mustangs are usually shown in positions of violent action. (See Fig. 56.)

This most popular of all temperamental horses is shown trying to unload his rider (Figs. 57 and 58). It was one of my earliest horse-and-rider combinations and made of light mahogany. The man is attached to the horse by one hand, two knees and the boots. The grain runs vertically to gain strength in all but the right front leg, and this one must be carefully handled. To help this situation, the legs are not separated until the final stages. In finishing the right leg, one finger is used to back up the foot while cutting on it (Fig. 59). The fingers must be trained to back up cutting pressure on parts, with the same delicate touch as that of a piano or flute player. Note there is no saddle or harness shown.

Fig. 57.

Fig. 58.

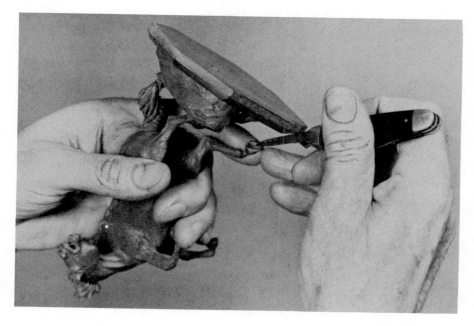

Fig. 59.

49

Again, here is an exciting and extremely active fellow (Figs. 60, 61, and 62) who is defiant of someone. Made of dark mahogany with grain running from extreme hind leg diagonally to the top of his head, the vulnerable parts during the cutting were the front legs and the tip of the tail. This one was full of bulging muscles because of the great tenseness and alertness of the body. With the head turned, we have a body that is not in any way symmetrical. Note that the hair flies out in a horizontal plain indicating the sweeping movement of the head. The whip of the tail, which adds to the horse's action, was a very fragile job that continually presented a challenge to keep in one piece. Here again, the

Fig. 60.

Fig. 61.

forelegs were the last to shape and detail, demanding great care and delicate gripping in order to prevent breakage when cutting. Over 90 hours of nerve-wracking work went into making it, but it was worth it.

It will be noted here that many of my more active models, especially mustangs, are supported on but two of their legs, indicating some

Fig. 62. Here and in Fig. 61 above are two views of the same excitable fellow.

Fig. 63.

kind of violent motion (Fig. 63). You have the immediate feeling that the other two, although raised, must come down and thus the motion is apparent. This one was among the earlier models, improved and more realistic in detail and construction. This fellow is leading with his left foot.

Here is shown the profile (Fig. 64), cut from red mahogany just

Fig. 64.

Fig. 65.

prior to carving. First the positions of the right and left legs are determined and cut away on opposite sides. The figure is quite symmetrical and the twist of the body action is no problem. This work required about 75 hours. The direction of the wood grain is here most important. The strength required in the two rear legs demanded that the grain runs with the position of the rear legs.

Since the subject is symmetrical, the modelling is normal. The importance of studying anatomy and muscle arrangement in order to get correct modelling contour cannot be stressed too much. When you understand the position of the skeletal bones, and the function and shape of the various muscles, you will be able to fashion the contour of the parts. Later in this book can be found some details on anatomy, particularly muscles.

A typical position of a mustang is to buck and kick (Figs. 65, 66, 67 and 68). This fellow, shown in Fig. 66, is made of a beautiful red cherry

53

Fig. 66.

wood, hard to cut in the rough stages, but enjoyable to finish. This one is among the best of my modelling jobs, and has a good swing and rhythm of motion. Here the grain runs diagonally from forefeet to tail, in order to gain strength in the supporting forelegs. The problem of cross-grain cutting requires great care in cutting the rear legs. Therefore, they will be the last to cut in the finishing stages.

Fig. 67.

Fig. 68. Note support between legs to protect them while detail is completed.

I actually started the cutting on the body and front section: head, neck and forelegs. Details of the hair and tail were left until the last.

One must always observe the rule "look at the rear legs when working on the front legs." This means that you must always be conscious of the shape and proportion of one part when working on another. If you become serious about making good horse models, get some facts on anatomy and continually study and refer to these details as you carve your horse. I cannot emphasize too strongly the value of basic knowledge.

One last detail about finishing. Rough-cut the rear legs to a general shape and finish the detailing of the hoof and fetlock assembly first. Then you can cut the shins and knee sections, working up to the body proper. As stated before, detail the hair and tail and eye parts last.

As you progress, you will commence to "feel" the proper proportion of the animal.

Some years ago I would visit the art exhibits in Carnegie Museum and spend an hour or two studying the priceless collection of ivory carvings. I would stand there and dream of how grand it would be to

Fig. 69.

Fig. 70.

have the ability to do something like that myself. I suppose that was the basis of my subsequent urge to carve. During my more productive years, I couldn't wait to get at my knife and a block of wood. Subconsciously a carving career had been germinating which, in later years, had sprouted and grown.

A very early model (Figs. 69 and 70) was cut from balsa wood in

Fig. 71. Front.

Fig. 72. Rear.

Fig. 73.

order to get a rough chiselled look. It was not shaved to a smooth surface as most others shown here were. This is not especially good modelling or detailing. (See also Figs. 71−78)

The drawings shown here were selected, from many that were used to cut the models shown on the preceding pages. Mustangs, even

Fig. 74.

Fig. 75.

when tamed, are active, jumpy and often contrary; thus, they should be designed with the busy, angular lines of motion.

The jumper in Fig. 74 was made from a very splintery deck mahog-

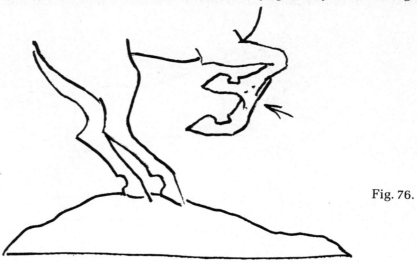

Fig. 76.

Fig. 77.

any and was relatively easy to cut. The front legs are out straight, but when landing, one will lead and touch down first. Figs. 75 and 76 show how good action can be found with the horse on two legs.

The mustang Indian pony (Figs. 78 and 79) is shown in a very springy canter, again supported on one leg, with the other rear leg connected by a raised section of wood. The front legs, the hair and the tail were cut across the grain. It is characteristic of a mustang bucking

Fig. 78.

and jumping. This is a most graceful flow of lines, with the positions of legs, neck and tail all indicating the rhythmic motion of the canter.

The rear and front legs were only roughly cut to finished dimension to maintain strength while working on the other parts, and fully detailed as the last part of the work. The head and body were completely detailed first. The rear legs were next and the forelegs were now completed. Eyes, hair detail and hoofs were the last to be done.

Polo Pony

Polo is an ancient game, possibly developed by the Hindus and the Persians centuries ago. The Indian name "pulu" became polo. The game further progressed in England where it became a sport for the rich, because they could afford the mounts for frequent substitution. The best polo horses are crossbred Thoroughbreds and cow ponies or Quarter Horses. They have been taught to move fast, stop, wheel and move rapidly in any direction. Horse and rider must cooperate perfectly. Here

Fig. 79.

are four of a team: The first (Fig. 79) is made of red mahogany, Fig. 80 was made of walnut, Fig. 81 is cherry, and Fig. 82 is light mahogany. In each one there is some delicate cross-grain cutting. Note that I do not try to detail too much harness or trappings, emphasis being on the coordinated action of horse and rider. Each model required about 65 hours.

Many times it will be apparent that a polo pony gets into a rocking motion when slowing up. The walnut model here tries to show that motion with each pair of feet moving almost together. This seldom produces good body rhythm. Note that the left rear foot is almost separated from the base. The drawing called for separation but it eventually appeared too risky. The grain runs diagonally with the lines of the rear leg. This required cross-grain cutting for the body and neck.

The delicate extremities such as a leg or tail of Figs. 83 and 84 can be backed up by a finger tip to absorb cutting pressure. This model required about 80 hours. Fig. 85 is a top view of Fig. 84.

Fig. 80.

Fig. 81.

Fig. 82.

Fig. 83.

Fig. 84.

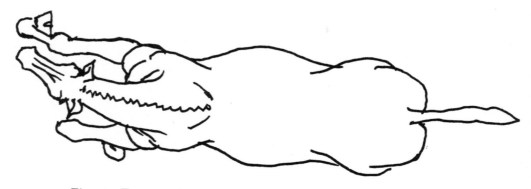

Fig. 85. Top view.

Fig. 86. Percheron and performer.

Percheron (Heavyweight)

Perhaps the most famous of this breed are found in the circus ring. They are sometimes known as "Rosinbacks" because of the rosin rubbed on their backs before they enter the ring. Originally brought from La Perche, France, they now are used for hauling and farm work, but their specialty is prancing around the circus ring. The center of Percheron breeding, today, is in Wayne, Illinois. They are mostly white or dappled grey and easily trained to trot to the waltz or two-step music of the circus band (Figs. 86, 87, 88 and 89).

Fig. 87.

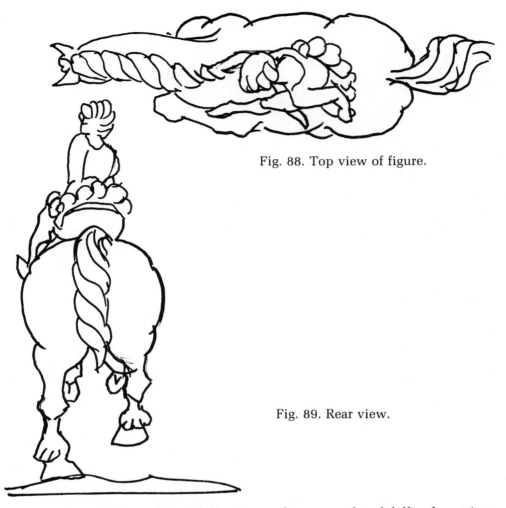

Fig. 88. Top view of figure.

Fig. 89. Rear view.

A good piece of straight-grain maple was used and difficult cutting produced the usual crop of finger blisters and cuts. The tight-grained wood held the minute edges well, and was a delight to finish. Continual shaving gave the whole model a smooth appearance. It would be a sin and a shame to use sandpaper. A two-tone appearance was caused by using wax on the body and rider and applying oil to the hair and tail and fetlocks. By balancing the horse on one toe, a rocking motion was indicated.

67

Fig. 90.

Since the design does not have delicate fragile parts the cutting was done progressively all over, permitting instant observance of proportion of parts. The figure of the lady was kept small to make the horse look larger.

This fellow is not as fragile as most of the others in my collection. The usual anxieties of possible breakage were not big problems. The position of the horse is symmetrical and thus the main worry was proper muscle bulge and arrangement.

Fig. 91.

An unusual pose (Figs. 90 and 91) and an unusual wood together add up to a fine example of rhythm in horse motion. Made of curly buckeye, it was a real challenge to cut into any kind of reasonable shape. Curly buckeye does not respond to carving strokes as an even-grain wood does. The grain has a deep marcel, which at any time takes a dip and leaves a wavy pattern. This means that careful cross-grain cutting is the only way to produce an intended surface. Every cut is a major operation. No one has faced real carving hazards until he has worked with curly buckeye. Four models similar to this one were made of this buckeye, each requiring about 80 hours.

Two models are shown (Figs. 92 and 93), both of which are stylized, not intended to be natural positions. Since they are both of

Fig. 92.

Fig. 93.

sturdy proportions, the cutting was progressively done, beginning with the body, and each leg and neck was cut a little here and a little there, and gradually the proportions of the parts could be evaluated. As said before, when cutting on one part, the eye should be aware of the relative shape of the others.

On these models, emphasis is placed on muscular shape, good detail of hoofs, fetlocks and fetlock "feathers"—the hair on the fetlocks. The eyes, nostrils, curving hair and tail should also be well detailed, adding to the excitement of the action.

Belgian

A compact animal (Figs. 94, 95 and 96), the Belgian has powerful hindquarters. Credit is often given to the humid soil of Belgium and the rich grass for his strength. Often used in the Middle Ages as a battle charger, the breed naturally became a farm horse, where it excels today in this country. This cherry model is swinging its short, heavy legs in a trot, which is top speed for its muscular body. Cherry takes longer, about 90 hours, but all the blisters and cuts are worth it when the finished animal is oiled to a deep red.

The cutting, starting with the profile cutout (Fig. 96), is slow, cherry being a tight-grained hardwood. Here again, the model should be progressively carved, keeping the eye on the progressive proportions of each part as the work develops. Too much cannot be said about the study of muscle action and anatomy in order to know what the outside contour should be.

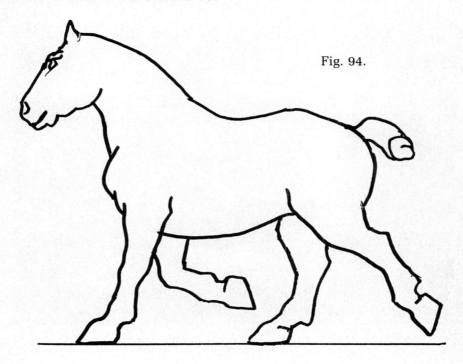

Fig. 94.

Fig. 95 (top) and Fig. 96 (bottom).

Shire

This is possibly the biggest and broadest horse known, weighing over a ton. (See Figs. 97 and 98.) The "feathers" on his legs were said to protect him from the sharp grass in the marshy fens of Lincolnshire, England. Largely used in early forests to drag logs and to pull great loads in western American grain belts, he has become a symbol of bigness on farms. This carving, too, was made of cherry, with the usual problems of this hardwood. The close grain holds detail well. Total time was about 70 hours.

The early stages of cutting cherry are rough when only knives are used, but the finishing is a joy, since cherry holds the edges of the grooves and contours.

Fig. 97.

Fig. 98.

Lipizzaners

A compact, powerful and exceedingly graceful animal, the Lipizzaner is often called "the ballet dancer." They are trained to perform a routine of difficult tricks, such as leaping, pirouetting and unusual kicking (Figs. 99 and 100 show the Capriole). A very old breed, they were originally crossbred from Arab stallions and Spanish mares and became pure white in color. The rider sits erect and his communication with the horse is not evident to the spectator. This breed was almost lost in World War II when the Nazis hid the whole Lipizzaner herd in Czechoslovakia, and General George S. Patton later provided a way of escape back to the American Zone in Austria.

Among the many Old World gavottes and mazurkas these white dancers perform are three more commonly known figures shown here. The first, the Capriole, is a springing leap which when complete finds all four legs stretched out like those of a flying Pegasus. This is one of the more sturdy models, made of dark walnut, and reflects the strength

Fig. 99.

of the animal. The hair and tail are arranged to indicate the jerky leaps being made. Also note the rigid posture of the rider, who may be communicating a signal to the horse, but no one can detect it. As usual, walnut is a very firm wood to detail.

Another well-known performance of the Lipizzaner is the Courbette, shown here in a drawing in Fig. 101. A model of this one was made of light mahogany and it, too, has the muscular look of the sturdy animal. To complete a Courbette, the horse is trained to balance on his hind legs and take successive leaps or hops. It takes a strong,

Fig. 100.

well-disciplined animal to do this, but the Lipizzaner is trained all of its life to perform these unusual movements. Fig. 101 is made of Honduras mahogany, a relatively easy wood to carve. The tail touching the ground provides a third support.

Fig. 101.

Another similar performance is the Levade, where the horse crouches on his hind legs very low and slowly raises his body to a 45 degree angle, not to a standing position. This cannot be done by any other horse, and the best of this breed cannot hold the pose longer than 10 to 15 seconds. A model was not made of this one.

Fig. 102.

Saddle Horse

Fig. 102 shows a very stylish four-gaited horse, made of dark mahogany, oiled to accentuate the dark red color of the wood. It was carved full-round, detailed from a desirable photograph, almost perfect as an illustration of slow gait. With cross-grain to contend with, the left front leg and the right rear leg were very carefully shaped. Here is a very good example of the importance of carefully placing your design on wood and allowing the grain to run in the direction where strength is needed.

These two legs are the last to be detailed. In this delicate cutting, back pressure is supplied by the forefinger, while the thumb and two middle fingers grip the solid parts of the body. Very frequently, cross-grain cutting is necessary for some of the parts of the model.

Fig. 103.

Fig. 104.

Fig. 105. Top view.

Tennessee Walker

One of the smoothest riding horses of any riding class, this horse gives his rider the feeling of being on a magic carpet (Figs. 103, 104 and 105). He has three gaits: the slow, flatfoot walk, the running walk and the faster rocking-chair canter. The origin of this breed is said to be a mixture of thoroughbreds, Morgans and standard breeds which were brought over the mountains to Tennessee by circuit riders, travelling preachers and other early adventurers from Virginia and the Carolinas. Long, rough-riding excursions developed a combination of stamina, easy strides and good manners from the original breeds which were the background of these walking horses from Tennessee.

The model shown here was made of a very hard walnut, and produced several of the worst cutting accidents to my left hand. For example, while undercutting the belly area, I ran about ½ inch of blade into the thumb side of my hand and later slashed the left forefinger fairly deeply. I am reminded of these and other cuts every time I look at this fellow.

Diagonal legs work in unison, with the left forefoot touching down slightly ahead of the right rear foot, and the rear foot coming down ahead of the forefoot point. These long strides are the secret of the smooth riding comfort. Note that the head is slightly turned, but the rest of the body is symmetrical. Emphasis is again placed on the necessity of studying the actual position of each hoof in the running or trotting movements of the horse. This model required about 95 hours to make.

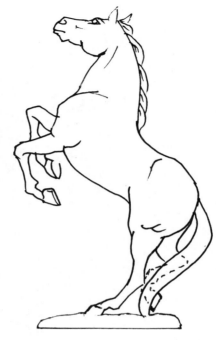

Fig. 106.

Thoroughbred

From Arab and Turk speed and stamina came the original stallion stock that was brought to England to become the fastest horse ever known. He is a very sensitive animal, a born racer with ancient Oriental ancestry (Fig. 106). He is credited with a stout heart and a stubborn desire to keep going in spite of trouble. About 1900, after Daniel Boone had promoted the breed in Kentucky, some American jockeys shortened the stirrups and rode high up on the horse's neck, providing the fast runner with even greater speed.

Figs. 106 and 107 show a typical jumpy pose of the breed when in defiance of something they do not understand or do not like. It was intended to be different than the average pose of a thoroughbred. It was cut from dark walnut, with a slight twist in the body which created some interesting problems of body balance. Note that he is actually standing on one hind leg, having some support from the end of the tail

Fig. 107.

Fig. 108.

and the tip of the left hind hoof. The grain runs vertically, causing some cross-grain cutting in the forelegs. In addition, some problems were caused by some hard burl patterns, which slowed up the job and made it require about 90 hours to finish.

Here is a running position (Figs. 108, 109 and 110) cut from light

Fig. 109. Because the grain of the wood does not run always with the position of the legs, it is important to keep a small portion of wood connecting the two legs until the hoof detail is complete.

mahogany. For interest, he also is resting on one leg with the lifted leg connected to the base and not quite fully separated. Flying rear legs became a problem to finish, and they were the last to detail. Here is a good swing to the action, showing the graceful movements of a fast animal. In each of my models, I try to introduce something other than a normal placid look. Some of the well-known thoroughbred champions are Man-o-War, Black Gold and War Admiral.

   The drawing is one of the many preliminary sketches of a series. The grain runs diagonally from the head to the rear hoofs, and thus the body parts are all cross-grain cutting.

Fig. 110.

COLTS

It was inevitable that the small fry be a part of the collection, and here is a two-week-old foal who is all legs. I made several models over this pattern of light mahogany and walnut (Figs. 111, 112, 113 and 114). In Figs. 113 and 114 it is posed on one leg, and as usual problems are caused in cutting the free legs. It has the appearance of bouncing and awkwardly springing along. By placing it on one rear leg, it is evident that good motion is developed.

Fig. 111.

Fig. 112. Top view.

With a small amount of material in the finished model, great care must be used in developing good proportion. Mistakes can easily ruin the job, and I've made some, but my German ancestry has taught me to salvage everything possible.

The mini-model of two-day-old foals staggering (Figs. 115 and 116) is about as tiny as one can go with wood. They are about one inch

Fig. 113.

Fig. 114.

high, made of dark mahogany, and oiled to keep a dark color. Eyes, feet and hair cannot be too detailed, but the try gives one a better feeling for these details in larger models. The lariat hanging on the post is a short length of string, varnished to hold a rigid coil. Great care must be taken on these very small models.

Fig. 115.

Fig. 116.

MIXED GROUP

A yearling colt and a mascot goat (Figs. 117, 118 and 119) proved to be the most difficult of all the models in the collection: first, the problem of two animals from one block and second, the endless trouble with curly buckeye, mentioned previously. Positioning the front legs to allow the colt to graze required some observation. The leggy fellow makes a fitting companion for the short stubby goat. The wood and its

Fig. 117.

Fig. 118.

peculiarities are described earlier in this book. Needless to say, with the wood problems always a threat of disaster, the cutting required to separate the two animals was most tedious and seemingly endless. Here again, all finishing was done by carefully shaving the surface of the wood.

Fig. 119. Top view.

SPECIAL
APPLICATIONS

This group of carvings represents a different technique of cutting. Here, the complete round of the model becomes more or less an outline for the profile, which is accented in depth by shadow lines and highlight areas. Most carvers use motor tools and chisels, but mine are cut with various blades of my hand knives. The first model (Figs. 120, 121 and 122) has been mounted in a frame, the picture part being basically dark mahogany. The lighter horse was cut from a laminated layer of white pine and the base part was cut from a laminated strip of dark

Fig. 120.

Fig. 121.

walnut. Fig. 122 shows the first stage—the basic cutting on mahogany. White pine was laminated above the right-hand horse. A base strip was later applied below the horses with walnut. Great care was used in preventing any undercuts because several porcelain castings were made from it and the slightest undercut will prevent the release of the plaster mould.

Fig. 122.

The graceful lines of Fig. 121 formed the basis for the carving that was cast later into a porcelain plaque. White pine, mahogany and walnut were laminated to produce a multi-color effect.

The horse-head plaque (Fig. 123) is a portrait of a famous Lipizzaner horse, Siglava Monterosa. He was copied from a picture found in Major Podhajsky's book, *The White Stallions of Vienna*. The cutting is not deep and it is suitable for moulding and porcelain- or plaster-casting. I keep these plaques waxed in order to apply a lubricant should a clay moulding be desired at any time. The wood was white pine.

Fig. 123.

The plaque in Fig. 124 was deeply cut and somewhat undercut for greater modelling. It is a deep red mahogany, oiled to keep the dark color. It would require a rubber mould if copies are ever made. A deep-set shadow-box frame was made to set off this deep relief and it was placed in the Admissions Office of Seton Hill College in Greensburg, Pennsylvania.

The horse-head drawing (Fig. 125) was carefully copied from a picture, and after several tracings were made this one was considered a fairly accurate portrait of a famous Lipizzaner horse. These horses are pure white, lending themselves to white pine or birch.

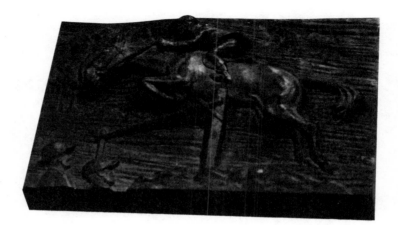

Fig. 124.

Fig. 125.

Fig. 126.

The drawing (Fig. 126) was one of many traced of a horse and rider
to show the actual clearance of an obstacle, with the horse's hind legs
touching the brush. When made in the wood, the rail was used and the
horse is still rising to clear it.

The cowboy (Fig. 127) is an interesting arrangement that was cut
on a diamond-shaped piece of light mahogany, with the bottom point
supported on a suitable base, making it a free-standing plaque.

These two wild, exciting subjects made excellent plaques, having
many angular and opposing lines of motion. The broncobuster in Fig.

Fig. 127.

128 was made into an outline, single-line cutting and Fig. 130 was a deep-cut relief in mahogany. Both were made entirely with knives, but rotary cutting equipment can be used on the outline. An interesting sketch (Fig. 129) could be made into a relief carving with some lively action and a lot of outline detail. White pine or mahogany is suggested.

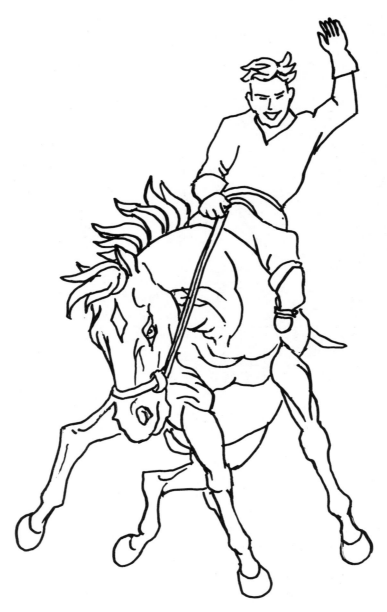

Fig. 128.

Fig. 129.

Fig. 130.

Fig. 131.

The Indian group in Fig. 131 was cut in red mahogany and oiled to keep the rich red color. The idea came from sketches made of a statue, but details are not available. Here is some really wild action. The two sketches in Figs. 132 and 133 are variations made up from sketches used in making up full-round models described elsewhere. They could be made up into bookends.

Ornaments

Of the many horse heads cut at one time or another the walnut model of Fig. 134 was developed further than any other. It was moulded and cast into bronze and aluminum, from both sand and match-plate moulds.

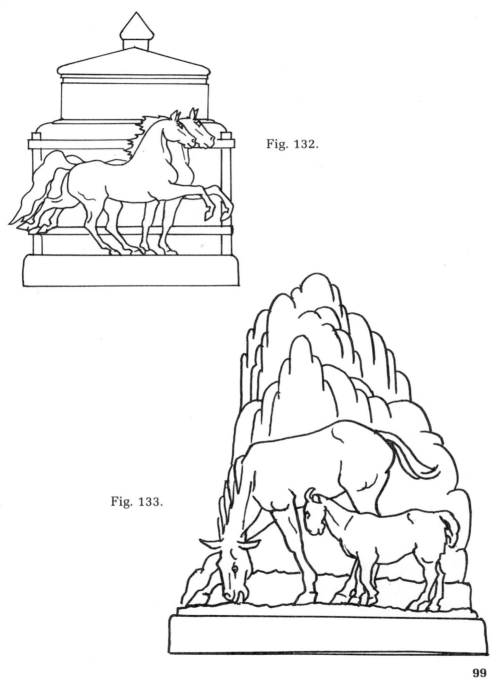

Fig. 132.

Fig. 133.

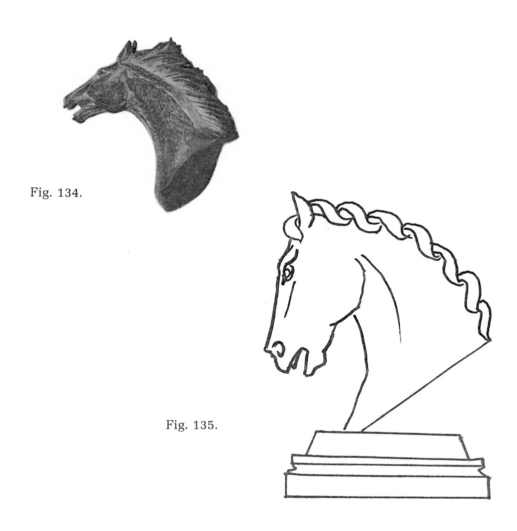

Fig. 134.

Fig. 135.

Fig. 135 was not moulded. The drawing in Fig. 136 shows an application to a cylindrical pedestal such as a trophy arrangement. Many of these were mounted on small marble bases and used as ornaments or paperweights. Others were suggested as ornaments on heavy, raised-center ash trays and some for box-cover ornaments. Note that the wild attitude was derived from the open mouth and the flowing hair.

100

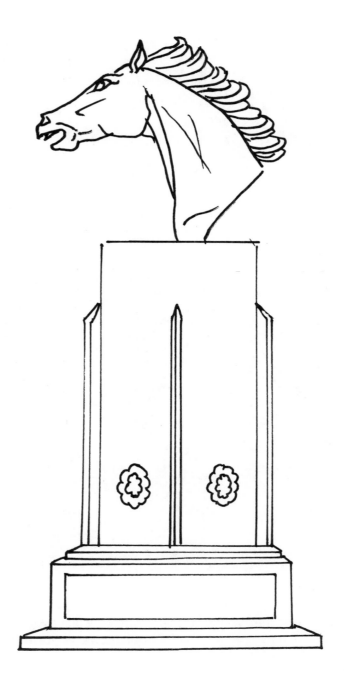

Fig. 136.

Fig. 137.

The very elaborate design of Fig. 137 was never made up, but it is shown to illustrate the extent of imaginary doodling.

Fig. 138.

An interesting application of the horse head that is shown in Fig. 138 was this idea and several others that were made for suppliers of desk equipment.

The drawings shown in Figs. 139 and 140 are of patterns made up for door knockers. Fig. 139 was sand-moulded and cast in bronze, as was a similar arrangement. The arrangement of Fig. 140 was developed into a white pine pattern and has made an excellent and popular door knocker in bronze. The photo (Fig. 141) shows how the white pine model was cast into brass and used for many gifts.

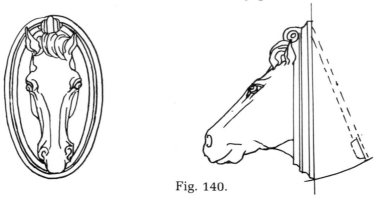

Fig. 139.   Fig. 140.

Fig. 141.

Bookends

An endless number of bookend designs can be made from sketches used in cutting full-round models (Fig. 142). A few are shown here, some in bas-relief and one full-round carved horse in white pine (Fig. 143). The latter is working hard at performing his task of holding up books.

In making up models of this sort, one must keep in mind the undercutting of the horse. The tendency is to try reproducing the finished article in bronze or porcelain. I did not mention epoxy because I have had little experience with it and what I did try turned out to be a failure. Some undercutting can be permitted if a rubber or fish-glue mould is to be made. I stick to clay moulding for porcelain castings and rubber moulds for brass casting (lost-wax process).

The Percheron in the model in Fig. 143 was cut and waxed without the upright against his knees as shown in the sketch. He looked much better with his knees in the clear, holding the book upright. Someday I will make a rubber mould and have some bronze castings made.

104

Fig. 142.

Again I wish to point out that no sandpaper or emery is ever used in the finishing of any kind of carving. Sometimes small cutting impressions are desirable to provide a textured look. If a more polished look is desirable, I carefully shave it a little smoother.

Fig. 143.

I've used many kinds of wood for the models and find that maple or cherry make up the best-looking finished models. The models in Figs. 144 and 146 were finished in a smooth-grain maple. One reason for this choice is that, when waxed, the grain hardly shows in any strong pattern, and I like these better that way.

Fig. 144.

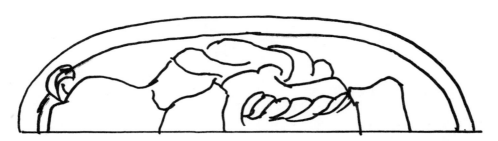

Fig. 145. Top view.

Fig. 146.

Sectional Wall Plaque

A more complicated project was a 22-inch-high mosaic-type bucking
bronco and rider in a wild, jumping motion. Twenty-two pieces of
various colored woods such as walnut, mahogany, white pine and
birch were used to produce an interesting assembly shown in Fig. 147.

Fig. 147.   Fig. 148.

On the next few pages will be shown a few of the general arrangements and working drawings. The outline is an enlargement of the model described previously.

Each of the many pieces was first cut in profile and roughly shaped. Then they were fitted and carefully finished for joining. Each piece was dowelled horizontally and glued and allowed to dry. When all the pieces were together (Fig. 147) the complete assembly was screwed down to a dark walnut base which was made one inch wider than the general outline of the complete model. The completed model was then heavily varnished.

When the sectional parts for the mosaic are determined, each is numbered for individual cutting, fitting (Fig. 149), and developing in cross-sections of each. The model is visualized and the thickness of each piece established.

A general arrangement drawing of the horse and rider was used as a basis for all of the cross-sections and itemized sketches. The only material other than the several kinds of wood was the hemp rope snub rein, which was soaked in varnish to make it rigid when placed and allowed to dry.

109

Fig. 149.

Each of the cut pieces requires a marked-up sketch showing the thickness and kind of wood to be used. Outlines of each piece are traced on the required wood for cutting. After complete assembly, the

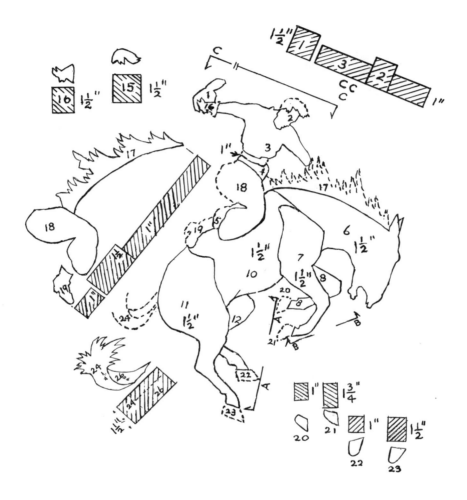

Fig. 150.

edges are rounded and detailing is completed, with many of the knife cuts left to provide a somewhat chiselled look. By using several kinds of wood, a color pattern can be established. Total cutting and mounting time is about 115 hours.

Carousel

A very ambitious undertaking was the design, cutting and assembly of a 22-inch-diameter carousel. The parts have all been cut, but the completion was delayed because of the lack of the right jive-waltz tune on a music box.

First, a small turntable was acquired and the speed changed from one revolution in about four seconds to about one revolution in eight seconds.

Complete drawings of all parts and assemblies were made and a bill of material made up so that all parts were available as work progressed. Several kinds of wood were used, such as maple, pine, mahogany and walnut; small mirrors were found; steel wire crown and pinion gears were formed and fitted and small hardwood rollers were made for tracking the animals (Fig. 150) in their reciprocating movement.

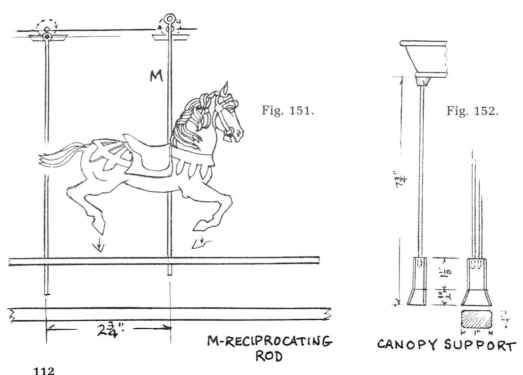

Fig. 151.

Fig. 152.

M—RECIPROCATING ROD

CANOPY SUPPORT

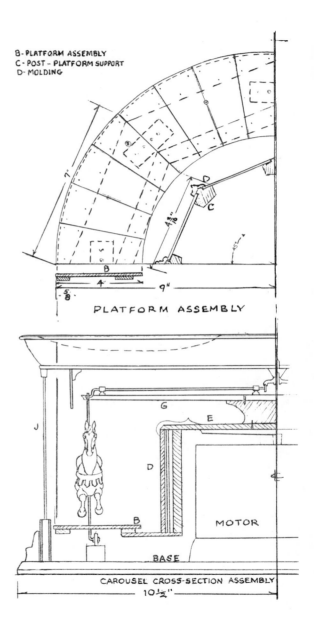

B- PLATFORM ASSEMBLY
C- POST - PLATFORM SUPPORT
D- MOLDING

PLATFORM ASSEMBLY

Fig. 153.

CAROUSEL CROSS-SECTION ASSEMBLY

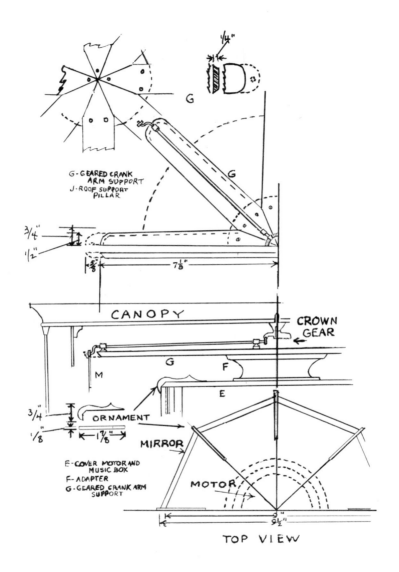

G

¼"

G - GEARED CRANK
ARM SUPPORT
J - ROOF SUPPORT
PILLAR

G

¾"

½"

⅝

7⅛"

CANOPY

CROWN
GEAR

G

F

M

E

¾"

ORNAMENT

⅛"

1⅞"

MIRROR

E - COVER MOTOR AND
MUSIC BOX
F - ADAPTER
G - GEARED CRANK ARM
SUPPORT

MOTOR

9½"

TOP VIEW

Fig. 154.

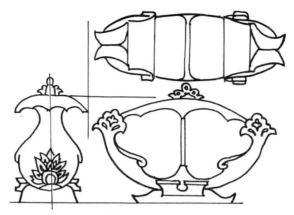

Fig. 155. Carriage.

Here are drawings (Figs. 151, 152, 153, and 154), giving further detail of the mounting arrangement of the reciprocating rod, crank and gear. A crown gear is mounted on the stationary top canopy and is fixed. As the platform and music-box assembly turn, a pinion gear on a steel-rod crank arm is rotated from the crown gear, and the crank moves the animal up and down. A roller and wavy track can also be attached to the lower end of the vertical shaft that supports the animal. The geared crank assembly can be eliminated and the carousel, with animals and sleighs in a fixed position, is still a great project to tackle.

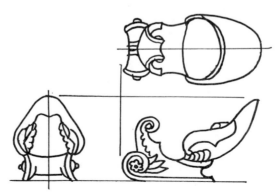

Fig. 156. Carriage.

The color scheme can be varied. I started with a basic white, with many light blue panels and an occasional edging or striping in red. Lavish use of gold for all the fancy scroll design and ornament is desirable. Trimmings on the harness and the carriages are gold highlighted. The platform can be stained in oak or walnut. Upright canopy supports. (Fig. 151) and steel rods should be gold-finished.

The carousel described here was designed to accommodate four animals and four carriages (Figs. 155, 156 and 157). This is as far as it can be simplified. The units can be increased in number as far as it is desirable, keeping in mind that they should be even in number to fit the four quarter sections of the platform.

The animals and carriages were made of lightweight pine and balsa.

The animal hair and tails can be black as well as the harness. The saddle blanket should be red, and the saddle brown, with lavish gold trim on all harness pieces. The animals can be white or light brown.

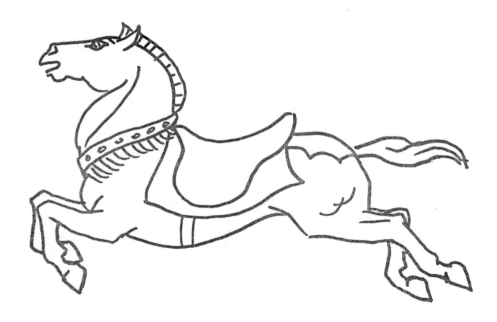

Fig. 157.

Fig. 157. (cont.)

REPLICAS

No doubt every carver has the desire to make some kind of reproduction of his work. I have been through it and have made up some porcelains and bronzes which were successful.

The first was a porcelain made from a carving shown previously. It was made from a clay moulding of a bas-relief (Fig. 158), shown earlier in wood. After testing for slight undercuts, the wood model was lubricated and moulded. I made several copies, this one in pure white porcelain and a few others in a combination of colored glaze finishes.

Fig. 158.

Fig. 159.

The second attempt was the bronze horse head, shown mounted on white marble in Fig. 159. This one was sand-moulded, but a number of later castings were made from a match-plate mould.

Among the many reproductions made from a wood model was this bronze wax-investment casting of a walnut Indian pony (Fig. 160). This is the hard way to do it because models intended for bronze

Fig. 160.

should be made of wax. With the grain running in line with the direction of the hind legs, they were broken in the process of mould-making. This is more serious than breaking a finger, for 75 hours were spent carving the wood.

The bronze casting was made from a rubber mould. It was cast in a Long Island foundry and, starting from a wood pattern, was quite expensive. The bronze mounted on red marble is one of my prizes. It is one of the rewards one realizes for a lot of long, hard work.

The next project will be an attempt to pour an epoxy casting, which with addition of bronze powder will make a fine little ornament, weighing about ⅙ as much as bronze.

Chariot

The tiny four-horse chariot (Figs. 161 and 162) shown earlier in Fig. 34 is detailed to scale. The chariot body is made of one piece with small insulated copper wire used as the boarding handle. The wheels may be cut from one piece, but it is more realistic to cut the hub, spokes and rims, then put it together. The rim should be made of straight-grain ash or fruitwood. The circumference of the wheel can be determined by multiplying the outside diameter by pi (3.1416). The rim strips should be boiled for quite a while, until soft enough to bend without breaking.

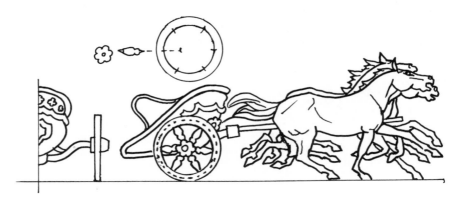

Fig. 161.

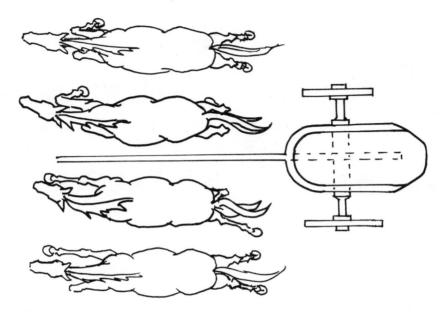

Fig. 162. Top view.

A heavier soft wire can be wrapped around the rim when assembled, twisted tight, and kept on until the glue is dry.

BUCKLES, PINS AND BUTTONS

Many interesting and useful things can be made up by using a little thought and imagination. By using the outline of a trained show horse in the various routine performances in competition, a fine series can be arranged. In this case, a fine-gaited gelding is shown (Figs. 163–167), all cut over the same basic pattern. They are especially attractive in walnut, cherry or some other dark wood that polishes well.

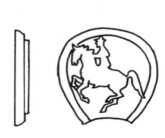

Fig. 163.

Fig. 164.

Figs. 165–167.

This series of carved horseheads for ornamental pins (Figs. 168 and 169) was cut in white pine, as I wished to make moulds and cast them with colored glazes in porcelain. The pin and clasp assemblies were taken from inexpensive jewelry and glued on the back of the pieces.

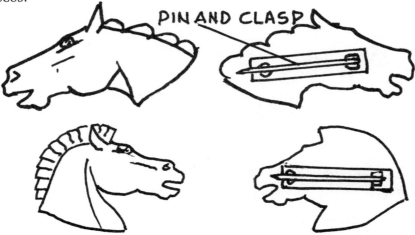

Figs. 168 and 169. Pins and clasps.

AFTERWORD

Now you can see why time means little to a carver. The thought occurred to me many years ago that some kind of evidence of progress could be recorded in order to show graphically what is actually cut off during each sitting (Fig. 170). I saved all the cuttings in separate piles and it was interesting to observe that, as the model was nearing completion, fewer and smaller chips were produced. In the final stages, much more deliberation is required for each chip and shaving. These separate piles accumulated in volume inversely as the total time increased.

Fig. 170.

It is not unusual to record from fifty to eighty hours on one model. There is no such thing as a time card for the true carver. His first and foremost thought concerns the degree of fidelity and quality of workmanship. When the carving is complete there can be no alteration, except in reduction if a part here and there will stand a little taken off. Unlike clay or oil painting, there can be no adding or shaping. The wood is cut so far, and work is stopped. Thus, we can assume that carving is a greater challenge for creative skill than many of the other arts.

If other wood carvers think as I do, they are their own most severe critics. In my own case, I have never completed one model that completely satisfied me. There is always some little thing that could be done better. This conclusion is carefully filed in the mind in hopes that it will influence a similar situation the next time it arises.

Other books have more elaborate information on woods and tools. My models have all been shaped with a choice of several hand knives. A motorized tool with a selection of cutters is more useful to me on bas-relief work. As stated before, the various kinds of wood each seem to have a distinctive personality. The more I work with wood, the greater my respect and affection for natural wood finishes. When my models are complete, I coat them with either linseed oil or liquid wax, depending on the degree of color I want. Oil darkens the grain, and with some woods it brings out an interesting pattern. Wax keeps the original tone in all but some soft woods. In my curly-buckeye models, wax finishing retains the ghostly grey color, and oil greatly accentuates the wavy marcel of the grain and considerable contrast of color.

My own taste forbids my painting or the addition of other materials, such as leather or metal. To me it is sacriligious to use sandpaper. I prefer knife finishing only, and have a few that have been shaved down to a relative smoothness. This is great when working with maple or cherry.

Occasionally someone asks me if I have exhibited to the public in any organized show. This is something I do not actively pursue, but I have accepted a few invitations. One of these exhibits produced several two-page rotogravure pictorial reviews in the *Pittsburgh Press*, Sunday Edition; the first on July 13, 1958 and the other on January 31,

1965. The exhibit that induced these stories was a hobby show in the window of the Mellon Bank in Pittsburgh, Pennsylvania. Many letters from friends resulted from this exhibit and, of course, were always warmly appreciated. Several other hobby shows and several art club shows were entered with a few ribbons received, one for best of show.

Some time ago, a winning ribbon in the handcraft section of a local church art show was received and, of course, appreciated. More recently the group was shown twice in the Butler Art Gallery in Youngstown, Ohio, the Seton Hill College Library in Greensburg, Pennsylvania and the Ligonier Library in Ligonier, Pennsylvania.

Because horses have been my specialty, I would like to suggest some things to look for when examining a carved or sculptured animal. First, look for good rhythm design and proportion of parts. Even in a standing model, the legs should not be stiff and duplicate in shape. The beast should have some indication of a natural, relaxed look with the head often slightly turned indicating that something has caught his interest.

Look for detail and expression of eyes and ears. Even his nostril should have some shape and not be just a slight gouge in the surface. Look for detail in the fetlocks, the hair on the neck and tail. The parting, or slight sway in the breeze makes these parts more interesting. Then, too, does he wear shoes if one or more feet are lifted?

If you are looking for over-simplified and impressionistic pieces, find one with some sort of good design, or my advice is to forget it.

As most of my horses are in motion, there is little symmetry in their design. I think of the axis of the shoulder joints and the hip joints as two horizontal bars supported and pivoted on a center pole—the spinal column. Then the front axis turns or drops from horizontal, then the rear axis must move in some corresponding related motion.

Any motion should have the look of effort and power exerted, even though the motion is not vigorous. Remember that the rhythm and harmony exhibited in the motion of active horses is as pleasing as good music. That is no doubt why the horse is popular, and this could be the reason that I carved so many of them.

BIBLIOGRAPHY

Alcock, Ann. *The Love of Horses:*   Octopus Books, Ltd.

Henry, Marguerite. *Album of Horses*. New York: Rand McNally.

McMillan, George. *The Golden Book of Horses*. New York:
    Golden Press.

Podhajsky, Alois. *The White Stallions of Vienna*. New York:
    E.P. Dutton and Co.

Remington, Frederic. *Frederic Remington's Own West*. New York:
    Dial Press, Inc.

Russell, Charles M. *Good Medicine*. New York: Garden City Pub. Co.

INDEX